D0438292

on inequality

inequality

HARRY G. FRANKFURT

Princeton University Press
Princeton and Oxford

Copyright © 2015 by Princeton University Press

Published by Princeton University Press
41 William Street, Princeton, New Jersey 08540

In the United Kingdom: Princeton University Press
6 Oxford Street, Woodstock, Oxfordshire OX20 1TW

press.princeton.edu

Library of Congress Cataloging-in-Publication Data

Frankfurt, Harry G., 1929–
  On inequality / Harry G. Frankfurt.
    pages cm
  Includes bibliographical references.
  ISBN 978-0-691-16714-5 (hardcover : alk. paper)
  1. Income distribution. 2. Distributive justice.
  3. Equality—Philosophy. I. Title.
  HB523.F73 2015
  340'.115—dc23   2015009807

British Library Cataloging-in-Publication Data
is available

This book has been composed in Sabon Next LT Pro
and Berthold Akzidenz-Grotesk

Printed on acid-free paper. ∞

Printed in the United States of America

10 9 8 7 6 5 4 3 2 1

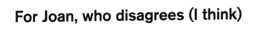

For Joan, who disagrees (I think)

contents

preface

There has recently been quite a bit of discussion—stimulated in part by the publication of the French economist Thomas Piketty's research[1]—concerning the growth in our society of economic inequality. The size of the gap between the economic resources of those who have more money and those who have less has been increasing rapidly. This development is regarded by many people as deplorable.

It is certainly true that those with greater wealth enjoy significant, and often objectionable, competitive advantages over those with less wealth. This is most conspicuous, of course, with regard to consumption. It is also conspicuous, far more importantly, with regard to social and political influence. The richer are in a position to throw around quite a bit more weight than are the poorer, in affecting the character of our social mores and conduct, and in determining the quality and the trajectory of our political life.

Insofar as economic inequality is undesirable, however, this is not because it is as such morally objectionable. As such, it is not morally objectionable. To the extent that it truly is undesirable, it is on account of its almost irresistible tendency to generate unacceptable inequalities of other kinds. These unacceptable inequalities, which may sometimes go almost so far as to undermine the integrity of our commitment to democracy, must naturally be controlled or avoided in the light of appropriate legislative, regulatory, judicial, and executive monitoring.

It is, I believe, of some considerable importance to get clear about these matters. Appreciating the inherent moral innocence of economic inequality leads to an understanding that it is misguided to endorse economic egalitarianism as an authentic moral ideal. Further, it facilitates recognition of why it may actually be harmful to regard economic equality as being, in itself, a morally important goal.

The first part of this book is devoted to a critique of economic egalitarianism. Its conclusion is that, from a moral point of view, economic equality does not really matter very much, and our moral and political concepts may be better focused on ensuring that people have enough. In the second part of the book I will recover one way in which economic equality may indeed be of some moral significance.

one

economic equality
as a moral ideal

First man: "How are your children?"
Second man: "Compared to what?"

I

1. In a recent State of the Union address, President Barack Obama declared that income inequality is "the defining challenge of our time." It seems to me, however, that our most fundamental challenge is not the fact that the incomes of Americans are widely *unequal*. It is, rather, the fact that too many of our people are *poor*.

Inequality of incomes might be decisively eliminated, after all, just by arranging that all incomes be *equally below* the poverty line. Needless to say, that way of achieving equality of incomes—by making everyone equally poor—has very little to be said for it. Accordingly, to eliminate income inequality cannot be, as such, our most fundamental goal.

2. In addition to the incidence of poverty, another part of our current economic disorder is that while many of our people have too little, quite a number of others have too much. The very rich have, indisputably, a great deal more than they need in order to live active, productive, and comfortable lives. In extracting from the economic wealth of the nation much more than they require in order to live well, those who are excessively affluent are guilty of a kind of economic gluttony. This resembles the gluttony of those who gobble down considerably more food than they need for either their nutritional well-being or a satisfying level of gastronomic enjoyment.

Apart from harmful psychological and moral effects upon the lives of the gluttons themselves, economic gluttony presents a ridiculous and disgusting spectacle. Taken together with the adjacent spectacle of a sizable class of people who endure significant economic deprivation, and who are as a consequence more or less impotent, the general impression given by our economic arrangements is both ugly and morally offensive.[1]

3. To focus on inequality, which is not in itself objectionable, is to misconstrue the challenge we actually face. Our basic focus should be on reducing both poverty and excessive affluence. That may very well entail, of course, a reduction of inequality. But the reduction of inequality cannot itself be our most essential ambition. Economic equality is not a morally compelling ideal. The primary goal of our efforts must be to repair a society in which many have far too little, while others have the comfort and influence that go with having more than enough.

Those who are much better off have a serious advantage over those who are less affluent— an advantage that they may tend to exploit in pursuing inappropriate influence over electoral and regulatory processes. The potentially antidemocratic effects of this advantage must be dealt with, accordingly, by legislation and regulation designed to protect these processes from distortion and abuse.

4. Economic egalitarianism is, as I shall understand it, the doctrine that it is desirable for everyone to have the same amounts of income and of wealth (for short, "money").[2] Hardly anyone would deny that there are situations in which it makes sense to deviate from this standard: for instance, where opportunities to earn exceptional compensation must be offered in order to recruit employees with skills that are badly needed but uncommon. However, despite a readiness to agree that some inequalities are permissible, many people believe that economic equality has, in itself, considerable moral value. They urge that

efforts to approach the egalitarian ideal should therefore be accorded a significant priority.[3]

In my opinion, this is a mistake. Economic equality is not, as such, of any particular moral importance; and by the same token, economic inequality is not in itself morally objectionable. From the point of view of morality, it is not important that everyone should have *the same*. What is morally important is that each should have *enough*. If everyone had enough money, it would be of no special or deliberate concern whether some people had more money than others.

I shall call this alternative to egalitarianism the "doctrine of sufficiency"—that is, the doctrine that what is morally important with regard to money is that everyone should have enough.[4]

5. The fact that economic equality is not in its own right a morally compelling social

ideal is in no way, of course, a reason for regarding it as being, in all contexts, an unimportant or an inappropriate goal. Indeed, economic equality may have very significant political or social value. There may be quite good reasons to deal according to an egalitarian standard with problems having to do with the distribution of money. Hence it may at times make sense to be more immediately concerned with attempting to increase the extent of economic equality than with trying to regulate the extent to which everyone has enough money.

Even if economic equality itself and as such is not important, commitment to an egalitarian economic policy might be indispensable for promoting the attainment of various desirable social and political ends. Also, the most feasible approach to reaching universal economic sufficiency might actually turn out to be, in fact, a pursuit of equality. That economic equality is not a good in itself leaves open the possibility, obviously, that it may be instrumentally valuable as a necessary condition for the attainment of goods that do genuinely possess intrinsic value.

So a more egalitarian distribution of money would certainly not be objectionable. Nevertheless, the widespread error of believing that there are powerful moral reasons for caring about economic equality for its own sake is far from innocuous. As a matter of fact, this belief tends to do significant harm.

6. It is often argued as an objection to economic egalitarianism that there is a dangerous conflict between equality and liberty. The argument rests on the assumption that if people are left freely to themselves, there will inevitably be a tendency for inequalities of income and wealth to develop. From this assumption, it is inferred that an egalitarian distribution

of money can be achieved and sustained only at the cost of repressing liberties that are indispensable to the development of that undesired tendency.

Whatever may be the merit of this argument concerning the relationship between equality and liberty, economic egalitarianism engenders another conflict, of more fundamental significance. To the extent that people are preoccupied with economic equality, under the mistaken assumption that it is a morally important good, their readiness to be satisfied with some particular level of income or wealth is—to that extent—not guided by their own most distinctive interests and ambitions. Instead, it is guided just by the quantity of money that other people happen to have.

In this way, economic egalitarianism distracts people from calculating their monetary requirements in the light of their own personal circumstances and needs. Rather, it encourages them to aim, misguidedly, at a level of affluence measured by a calculation in which—apart from their relative monetary situation—the specific features of their own lives play no part.

But, surely, the amount of money available to various others has nothing directly to do with *what is needed for the kind of life a person would most sensibly and appropriately seek for himself.* Thus a preoccupation with the alleged inherent value of economic equality tends to divert a person's attention away from trying to discover—within his experience of himself and of his life conditions—what he himself really cares about, what he truly desires or needs, and what will actually satisfy him.

That is to say, a preoccupation with the condition of others interferes with the most basic task on which a person's intelligent selection of monetary goals for himself most decisively depends. It leads a person away from understanding what he himself truly requires in order effectively to pursue his own most authentic needs, interests, and ambitions. Exaggerating the moral importance of economic equality is harmful, in other words, because it is *alienating*. It separates a person from his own individual reality, and leads him to focus his attention upon desires and needs that are not most authentically his own.

7. To be sure, noticing the economic circumstances of others may make a person aware of interesting possibilities. Furthermore it may provide data for useful judgments concerning what is normal or typical. A person who is attempting to reach a confident and realistic appreciation of what to seek for himself may well find this helpful.

Moreover, it is not only in suggestive and preliminary ways such as those that the economic situations of other people may be pertinent to someone's efforts to decide what monetary ambitions it would be most suitable for him to entertain. The amount of money someone requires may depend in a more direct way on the amounts of money that are available to others. Comparatively large amounts of money may—as is well known—bring exceptional power, or prestige, or other competitive advantages. Therefore, a calculation of how much money would be enough for a person cannot intelligently be made, if that person is likely to be engaged in a pertinent variety of competition, without consideration of how much money is likely to be available to those with whom the person may be required to compete.

The false belief that economic equality is important for its own sake leads people to separate the problem of estimating their proper monetary ambitions from the problem of understanding what is most fundamentally significant to themselves. It influences them to take too seriously, as though it were a matter of great moral concern, a question that is inherently rather insignificant and not directly to the point—namely, the question of how their economic status compares with the economic status of others. In this way the doctrine of equality contributes to the moral disorientation and shallowness of our time.

8. The prevalence of egalitarian thought is damaging in another way as well. It not only tends to divert the attention of people from considerations that are of greater moral or human importance to them than the question of economic equality. It also diverts the attention of intellectuals from the quite fundamental philosophical problems of understanding just what those more important considerations are, and of elaborating—in appropriately comprehensive and perspicuous detail—a con-

ceptual apparatus that might reliably guide and facilitate their inquiries.

Calculating the size of an *equal share* of something is generally much easier—a more straightforward and well-defined task—than determining how much a person needs of it in order to have enough. The very concept of having an *equal* share is itself considerably more transparent and intelligible than the concept of having *enough*. A theory of equality is much easier to articulate, accordingly, than a theory of sufficiency. The widespread appeal of economic egalitarianism has, unfortunately, masked the importance of systematic inquiry into the analytical and theoretical issues raised by the concept of *having enough*. Needless to say, it is far from self-evident precisely what the doctrine of sufficiency means, and what applying it entails. But this is hardly a good reason for adopting, in preference to it, an alternative that is incorrect.

II

9. There are a number of ways of trying to establish the false thesis that economic equality is actually important. For instance, it is sometimes argued that fraternal relationships among the members of society are desirable, and that economic equality is more or less indispensable for this. Or it may be maintained that inequalities in the distribution of money are to be avoided because they lead invariably to undesirable discrepancies of other kinds— for example, in social status, in political influence, or in the abilities of people to make effective use of their various opportunities and entitlements.

In both of these arguments, economic equality is endorsed because of its supposed importance in creating or in preserving certain noneconomic conditions. Considerations of this sort may well provide convincing reasons for recommending equality as a desirable social good. However, each of the arguments regards economic equality as valuable only *derivatively*—that is, as possessing value only on account of its contingent or instrumental connections to other things. Neither argument attributes to economic equality any unequivocally *intrinsic* value.

10. A rather different kind of argument for economic equality comes closer to regarding the value of that equality as being intrinsic. The argument—promulgated most notably by Professor Abba Lerner (of Columbia, the University of California–Berkeley, and the New School for Social Research)—is grounded on the principle of *diminishing marginal utility*. This principle of economics implies, it is maintained, that an equal distribution of money maximizes *aggregate utility*—the aggregated satisfactions of the members of society. That

is to say, given the total amount of money in a society, the aggregate utility provided by that money would be greater if the money were distributed equally than if it were distributed unequally.[5]

The argument depends on two assumptions: (a) for each individual, the utility of money invariably diminishes at the margin; and (b) with respect to money, or with respect to the things money can buy, the utility functions of all individuals are the same.[6]

Given the assumption both of (a) and of (b), it follows that a marginal dollar always brings less utility to a rich person than it would bring to a person who is less affluent.

This may appear to entail, further, that aggregate utility must increase when inequality is reduced by giving a dollar to someone who is less affluent than the person from whom it is taken, for the utility the recipient will acquire from the transfer will exceed the utility the donor will lose.

11. This further reasoning fails to take into account, however, the inflationary effect that is likely to be caused by taking money from the rich and giving it to the poor.[7] The supply of goods available for consumption does not increase, after all, when money is redistributed. On the other hand, the demand for certain goods by people who were formerly too poor to afford them is very likely to increase. Thus prices of those goods will probably rise.

This inflationary pressure will entail a corresponding reduction of consumption, perhaps not by the very rich—who will still have plenty of money with which to cope with the price increases—but by members of an intermediate class, who will be unable to maintain their accustomed level of consumption in the face of higher prices. The reduction of their standard of living will tend to offset the gain made by the formerly poor. This trade-off will mean that aggregate utility does not increase. The aggregate of utility cannot reliably be increased, then, by taking money from the rich and giving it to the poor.

12. In any event, the fact is that both (a) and (b) are false. In virtue of their falsity, the reasoning that links economic equality to the maximization of aggregate utility does not even get off the ground. The argument from diminishing marginal utility fails to render the desirability of redistributing money at all plausible.

So far as concerns (b), it is evident that the utility functions for money of different individuals are not even approximately alike. Some people suffer from physical, mental, or emotional weaknesses or incapacities that limit the levels of satisfaction they are able to enjoy. In addition to the effects of specific disabilities, some people simply enjoy things more heartily than other people do. Everyone knows that, at any given level of consumption, there are large differences in the utility derived by different consumers.

So far as concerns (a), there are strong reasons for not expecting any general decline in the marginal utility of money. That the marginal utilities of certain goods do indeed tend to diminish is clearly not an a priori principle of reason. It is a psychological generalization, based on the fact that our senses characteristically lose their freshness as a consequence of repetitive stimulation: after a time, people tend to be satiated with what they have been consuming. It is common knowledge that experiences of many kinds become increasingly routine and unrewarding as they are repeated.[8]

It is questionable, however, whether this provides any reason at all for expecting a diminution in the marginal utility of money—that is, of something that functions as a generic instrument of exchange. Even if the utility of everything money can buy were inevitably to diminish at the margin, the utility of money itself might nonetheless exhibit a different pattern. It is quite possible that money would be exempt from the phenomenon of unrelenting marginal decline, because of its limitless versatility.

From the supposition that a person tends to lose interest in what he is consuming as his consumption of it increases, it cannot be concluded that he must also tend to lose interest in consumption itself, or in the money that makes consumption possible. No matter how tired he has become of what he has been doing, there may always remain for him untried goods to be enjoyed, and, even if the availability of untried goods is finite and becomes exhausted, there may be further satisfaction to be derived from goods of which he was once but is no longer sated, and whose utility for him has thus been revived.

13. In any case, there are numerous things of which people do not, from the very outset, immediately begin to tire. From certain goods, in fact, people derive more utility after sustained consumption than they can derive at first. There are circumstances in which appreciating or enjoying something actually depends on repeated trials having been already accomplished. Those trials serve as a kind of "warming up" process—an introduction that prepares a person for being able to derive a satisfaction he is otherwise unable to reach.

This is the situation whenever relatively little gratification is received, from the item or experience in question, until the individual has warmed up, or has acquired a "special taste" for it, or has become addicted to it, or has in some other way begun to respond fulsomely to it. The capacity for obtaining gratification is then smaller at earlier points in the sequence of consumption than it is at later points. In such instances, marginal utility does not decline. It actually increases.

Suppose it were true of everything, without exception, that a person will ultimately lose interest in it. This would mean that there is a point in every utility curve at which the curve begins a steady and irreversible decline. It cannot be presumed, however, that every segment of the curve must have a downward slope.

III

14. When marginal utility diminishes, it does not do so on account of any deficiency in the marginal unit. It diminishes just in vir-

tue of the position of that unit as the latest in a sequence. The same is true when marginal utility increases: the marginal unit has greater utility than its predecessors precisely on account of the consumer's earlier consumption of the latter.

When the sequence consists of units of money, what corresponds to the process of *warming up*—at least, in one pertinent and important feature—is the process of *saving*. Accumulating savings entails, as warming up also does, generating a capacity to derive, at some subsequent point, gratifications that are not derivable earlier.

It may at times be especially worthwhile for a person to save money, rather than to spend each dollar as it comes along, in virtue of the incidence of what may be thought of as utility "thresholds." Consider an item with the following characteristics: it is not fungible, it can provide a fresh and otherwise unobtainable

25

type of satisfaction, and it is too expensive to be acquired except by saving up for it. The utility of the dollar that finally completes a program of saving up for such an item may be greater than the utility of any dollar saved earlier in the program. It may even be greater than their combined utilities, when the utility provided by acquiring the last item is greater than the utilities that could have been derived if the money saved had been spent as it came in. In such a situation, the final dollar saved permits the crossing of a utility threshold. It does not merely add another unit of utility to the others. It creates a utility that encompasses the others and that is greater than their sum.

15. People tend to think that it is generally more important for them to avoid a certain degree of harm than to acquire a benefit of comparable magnitude. It may be that this preference is in part due to an assumption that

utility usually does diminish at the margin. For, on that assumption, the additional benefit provided by the marginal acquisition would have less utility than is provided by the item that would be lost by the harm.

It is interesting to note, however, that the tendency to place a lower value on acquiring benefits than on avoiding harms is sometimes reversed. When people are so miserable that they regard themselves as "having nothing to lose," they may well place a higher value on improving their condition than on avoiding the harm of becoming (to a comparable degree) even worse off. In that case, what is diminishing at the margin is not the utility of benefits but the disutility of harms.

In virtue of utility thresholds, an incremental or marginal dollar may have conspicuously greater utility than dollars that do not enable a threshold to be crossed. For example, a person who uses his spare money during a certain period for an inconsequential improvement in his routine pattern of consumption—perhaps, let us say, a slightly and almost imperceptibly better quality of meat for dinner every night—may derive much less additional utility in this way than by saving up the spare money for a while and then going to see an exciting ball game.

16. It is sometimes argued that, for anyone who is rational in the sense that he seeks to maximize the utility generated by his expenditures, the marginal utility of money must necessarily diminish. Professor Abba Lerner presents this argument as follows:

> The principle of diminishing marginal utility of income can be derived from the assumption that consumers spend their income in the way that maximizes the satisfaction they can derive from the good ob-

tained. With a given income, all the things bought give a greater satisfaction for the money spent on them than any of the other things that could have been bought in their place but were not bought for this very reason. From this it follows that if income were greater the additional things that would be bought with the increment of income would be things that are rejected when income is smaller because they give less satisfaction; and if income were greater still, even less satisfactory things could be bought. The greater the income, the less satisfactory are the additional things that can be bought with equal increases of income. That is all that is meant by the principle of the diminishing marginal utility of income.[9]

I believe that this argument is unsound. The level of satisfaction a person can derive from a certain good may vary considerably according to whether or not he also possesses certain other goods. The satisfaction obtainable from a given expenditure may therefore be enhanced if some other expenditure has already been made.

Suppose, for instance, that a serving of popcorn costs the same as enough butter to make the popcorn delectable. Now imagine a rational consumer, who adores buttered popcorn, who gets very little satisfaction from unbuttered popcorn, but who nonetheless prefers unbuttered popcorn to butter alone. This consumer will buy the unbuttered popcorn in preference to the butter alone, accordingly, if he must buy one or the other and cannot buy both.

Now suppose that this person's income increases, so that he can now buy both the popcorn and the butter as well. Then he can have something he enjoys enormously: his incremental income makes it possible for him to enjoy the buttered popcorn he adores. The satisfaction he will derive by combining the popcorn and the butter may very likely be much greater than the sum of the satisfactions he would be able to derive from the two goods taken separately. Here, again, is a threshold effect.

17. The threshold effect is particularly integral to the experience of collectors. When a collector obtains the item that finally completes a collection on which he has been working for years, he may quite naturally derive a satisfaction greater than that which he has derived from obtaining any (or all) of the other items in the collection, even if—taken by itself—that last item has no greater utility than does any of the other items.

Obtaining the final item may often entail, for a collector, crossing a utility threshold. A complete collection consisting of twenty items, each of which has the same utility when the items are considered individually, may have greater utility for the collector than an incomplete collection that is of the same size but that includes duplicates. This is because the completeness of the collection itself provides an additional utility acquired as the threshold is crossed—a utility that is in addition to the utility provided by the individual items of which the collection is composed.

In a case of this sort, it is not true that the marginal utility of the money the person uses to acquire $G(i)$ (the good he is able finally to acquire with the increased income) is less than the marginal utility of the money he used to acquire $G(n)$ (the goods that the rational consumer actually buys with his income of n dollars). When there is an opportunity to create a combination that is (like buttered popcorn) synergistic in the sense that adding one good to another results in more utility than the combined utility of each taken separately, the marginal utility of money may not decline even though the sequence of marginal items— taking each of these items exclusively by itself— may exhibit a pattern of declining utilities.

Lerner's argument is flawed in virtue of another consideration as well. It evidently presumes that what the consumer buys when his income is increased by i dollars must be something he could have bought earlier but rejected when his income was only n dollars. However, this presumption is unwarranted.

With an income of $(n + i)$ dollars, the consumer might use that income to obtain something too expensive for him to have afforded before his income increased. If a rational consumer with an income of n dollars defers obtaining a certain good until his income increases, this does not necessarily mean that he "rejected" obtaining it when his income was smaller. The good in question may have been out of his reach at that time simply because adding it to his other goods would have cost more than *n* dollars. His reason for postponing obtaining the item may have had nothing to do with comparative expectations of satisfaction, or with preferences or priorities at all.[10]

IV

18. The preceding discussion has established that an egalitarian distribution of income may fail to maximize aggregate utility. As a matter of fact, it can also be shown that there are conditions under which an egalitarian distribution actually minimizes aggregate utility.[11]

Thus suppose that there is enough of a certain resource (medicine, say, or food) to enable some but not all members of a population to survive. Let us stipulate that the size of the population is ten, that a person needs at least five units of the resource in question in order to stay alive, and that exactly forty units of the resource are available. At most, then, eight people can survive; and they can survive just by receiving a greater share of the essential resource than is received by the two individuals who will be left to die.

If any members of this population are to survive, then, some must have more than others. An equal distribution, which gives each person four units, leads to the worst possible outcome: namely, everyone dies. It would be morally grotesque, in a case of this sort, to insist that resources be shared equally!

It would also be unreasonable to maintain that, under the conditions specified, it is justifiable for some to be better off only—as some philosophers would claim—when this is in the interests of the worst off. Suppose that the available resources are sensibly distributed in such a way as to save eight people. The justification for doing this would obviously not rest on a belief that it somehow benefits the two members of the population who are left to die. Under conditions of exigent scarcity, when there is not enough to meet everyone's minimal requirements, the desirability of an egalitarian distribution may be quite out of the question.

19. Another response to scarcity is to distribute the available resources in such a way that as many people as possible have enough, or, in other words, that the distribution maximizes the incidence of sufficiency. But now suppose that, in the same example, there are available not just forty units of the vital resource but forty-one. Then, maximizing the incidence of sufficiency by providing enough for each of eight people leaves one unit unallocated. What should be done with this extra unit?

It has been shown above that it is a mistake to insist that, where some people have less than enough, no one should have more than anyone else: when resources are scarce, so that it is impossible for everyone to have enough, an egalitarian distribution may lead to disaster. It is also a mistake to claim that where some people have less than enough, no one should have more than enough. If this claim were correct, then—in the example at hand—the extra unit should not be used to provide more than enough to one of the people who otherwise has exactly enough to survive, but should be provided to one of the two people who have nothing.

The trouble with this alternative, clearly, is that one additional unit of the resource in question will not improve the condition of a person who has none. By hypothesis, that person will die even if given the extra unit. He does not need one unit. He needs five.[12] So the extra unit is of no particular use either to him or, in the circumstances, to anyone else. It might just as well simply be kept in reserve, or thrown away; or it might be given, in a supererogatory gesture, to one of the people who is already destined to survive.

It evidently cannot be taken for granted that a person who has a certain amount of a vital resource is necessarily better off than a person who has less; for the larger amount may still be too small—that is, not enough—to serve any useful purpose. Having the larger amount may even make a person worse off. Even if we suppose that a person with one unit of food or medicine may live a bit longer than someone with no food or medicine whatsoever, perhaps it is really worse to prolong the process of starvation or of illness for a short time than it would be to terminate sooner the foreseeable agony.

20. The idea that nobody should have more than enough while anybody has less than enough derives its plausibility from an assumption that is also plausible but that is nonetheless false: to wit, giving resources to people who have less than enough necessarily makes those people better off. It is indeed generally reasonable to assign a higher priority to improving the condition of those who are in need than to improving the condition of those who are not in any need. But giving additional resources to people who have less than enough of those resources, and who on that account are in serious need, may not actually improve the condition of those people at all.

It is important to notice that people who are below a certain utility threshold are not necessarily benefited by additional resources that move them closer to that threshold. What is crucial for them is to cross the threshold. Merely moving closer to it may fail to be of any help to them, or it may actually be disadvantageous.

By no means do I wish to suggest, of course, that it is never or only rarely beneficial to move closer to an important utility threshold without actually crossing it. It may certainly be beneficial, either because it increases the likelihood that the threshold will ultimately be crossed, or because—quite apart from the significance of crossing the threshold— additional resources may provide desirable increments of utility. Certainly, a collector may enjoy expanding his collection even if he believes that he has no chance of completing it.

V

21. Quite often, advocacy of egalitarianism is based less on an argument than on a pur-

ported moral intuition: economic inequality just seems wrong. It strikes many people as altogether apparent that, taken simply in its own right, the possession by some of more money than others is morally offensive.

I suspect that people who profess to have this intuition concerning manifestations of inequality are actually not responding to the inequality they perceive but to another feature of the situations they are observing. What I believe they find intuitively to be morally objectionable in circumstances of economic inequality is not that some of the individuals in those circumstances have less money than others. Rather, it is the fact that those with less have too little.[13]

When we consider people who are substantially worse off than ourselves, we do very commonly find that we are morally disturbed by their circumstances. What directly moves us in cases of that kind, however, is not a relative quantitative discrepancy but an absolute qualitative deficiency. It is not the fact that the economic resources of those who are worse off are smaller than ours. It is the quite different fact that their resources are too little. The fact about them that disturbs us is that they are so poor.

Mere differences in the amounts of money people have are not in themselves distressing. We tend to be quite unmoved, after all, by inequalities between those who are very well-to-do and those who are extremely rich. Our awareness that the latter are substantially better off than the former arouses in us no moral uneasiness at all.

If we believe of some person that his life is richly fulfilling, that he himself is genuinely content with his economic situation, and that he is not troubled by any resentments or sorrows that more money could assuage, we are not ordinarily much interested—at least, from a moral point of view—in a comparison of the amount of money he has with the amounts possessed by others. Economic discrepancies in cases of this sort do not impress us in the least as matters of significant moral concern. The fact that some people have much less than others is not at all morally disturbing when it is clear that the worse off have plenty.

22. The doctrines of egalitarianism and of sufficiency are logically independent: considerations that support the one cannot be presumed to provide support also for the other. Yet proponents of egalitarianism frequently suppose that they have offered evidence for their position when what they have in fact offered supports only the doctrine of sufficiency.

In attempting to gain acceptance of their doctrine, egalitarians often call attention to disparities between the conditions enjoyed by the rich and those suffered by the poor. It is

undeniable that contemplating such disparities does often elicit a legitimate conviction
that it would be morally desirable to redistrib-
ute the available resources so as to improve
the circumstances of the poor. And, of course,
that would bring about a greater degree of
economic equality. But the demanding moral
appeal of improving the condition of the poor
does not even tend to show that egalitarianism is, as a moral ideal, similarly demanding.

To show of poverty that it is compellingly
undesirable does nothing whatever to show
the same of inequality. What makes a person
poor in the morally relevant sense—in which
poverty is understood as a condition of serious economic deprivation—is not the fact of
having less money than others. Situations in-
volving inequality are morally disturbing, I
believe, only to the extent that they violate
the ideal of sufficiency.[14] This is confirmed, it
seems to me, by familiar discrepancies between

the principles egalitarians profess and the way in which egalitarians commonly conduct their own lives.

My point here is not that some egalitarians hypocritically accept high incomes and special opportunities for which, according to the moral theories they recommend, there is no adequate justification. The point is, rather, that many egalitarians (including many academic proponents of the doctrine) are not truly concerned about whether they themselves are as well off economically as are other people.

They often believe that they have roughly enough money for what is important to them, and they are therefore not terribly preoccupied with the fact that some people are considerably more affluent than they are. Many egalitarians would consider it rather shabby or even reprehensible to care, with respect to their own lives, about economic comparisons of that sort. And, notwithstanding the implications of the doctrine to which they adhere, they would be appalled if their children grew up with such concerns.

23. The fundamental error of economic egalitarianism lies in supposing that it is morally important whether one person has less than another, regardless of how much either of them has and regardless also of how much utility each derives from what he has. This error is due in part to the mistaken assumption that someone who has a smaller income has more important unsatisfied needs than someone who is better off. Whether one person has a larger income than another is, however, an entirely extrinsic matter. It has to do with a relationship between the incomes of the two people. It is independent both of the actual sizes of their respective incomes and,

more importantly, of the amounts of satisfaction they are able to derive from them. The comparison implies nothing at all concerning whether either of the people being compared has *any* important unsatisfied needs.

VI

24. What does it mean, at last, for a person to have enough? One thing it might mean is that any more would be too much: a larger amount would make the person's life unpleasant, or it would be harmful, or in some other way unwelcome. This sense is often what people have in mind when, especially in an angry or cautionary tone, they say such things as "I've had enough!" or "Enough of that!"

The idea conveyed by statements like these is that a limit has been reached, a limit beyond which it is not desirable to advance. On the other hand, the assertion that a person has enough may entail only that a certain requirement or standard has been met, with no implication that more would be bad. This is often what a person intends when he says something like "That should be enough." Statements such as this often characterize the indicated amount as sufficient, while leaving open the possibility that more might also be acceptable.

In the doctrine of sufficiency, the use of the notion of "enough" pertains to meeting a standard rather than to reaching a limit. To say that a person has enough money means— more or less—that he is content, or that it is reasonable for him to be content, with having no more money than he actually has. And to say this is, in turn, to say that the person does not (or cannot reasonably) regard whatever (if anything) is distressing or unsatisfying in his life as being due to his having too little money. In other words, if a person is (or ought reasonably to be) content with the amount of money he has, then insofar as he is or has reason to be unhappy with the way his life is going, he does not (or cannot reasonably) suppose that more (or, conceivably, less) money would enable him to become (or to have reason to be) significantly less unhappy with it.[15]

25. It is essential to understand that having enough money is far from being equivalent to having just enough to get by, or to having enough to make life marginally tolerable. People are not generally content with living on the brink. The point of the doctrine of sufficiency is not that the only morally important distributional consideration with respect to money is whether people have enough to avoid economic misery. A person who might naturally be said to have just barely enough does not really, according to the doctrine of sufficiency, have enough at all.

There are two distinct kinds of circumstance in which the amount of money a person has is enough—that is, in which more money will not enable him to become significantly less unhappy. On the one hand, it may be that the person is not at all unhappy; he is suffering no measurable distress or dissatisfaction with his life. On the other hand, it may be that although the person is indeed unhappy with how his life is going, the difficulties that account for his unhappiness would not truly be alleviated by more money.

Circumstances of this second kind obtain when what is wrong with the person's life has to do most particularly with noneconomic goods: for example, love, a sense that life is meaningful, satisfaction with one's own character, and so on. These are goods that money cannot buy. Indeed, they are goods for which none of the things money can buy are even approximately adequate substitutes.

Sometimes, to be sure, noneconomic goods are obtainable or enjoyable only (or more easily) by someone who has a certain amount of money. But the person who is distressed with his life may already have that much money. Since the unsatisfactory character of his life is not due to the size of his income or his wealth, his life would not be improved if he had more money.

It is possible that someone who is content with the amount of money he has might also be content with an even larger amount of money. Since having a large enough income does not mean being at a limit beyond which an income of a larger magnitude would necessarily be undesirable, it would be a mistake to assume that for a person who already has enough money the marginal utility of money must be either negative or zero.

Although this person is by hypothesis not distressed about his life on account of any lack of things that a larger income would enable him to obtain, it nonetheless remains possible that he would enjoy having some of those things. They would not make him less unhappy; nor would they in any way alter his attitude toward his life, or the degree of his contentment with it. However, they might bring him pleasure. If that is so, then his life would in that respect be better with more money than without it. The marginal utility for him of money would accordingly remain positive.

To say that a person is content with the amount of money he has does not entail, then, that there would be no point in providing him with more. A person who already has enough money might be quite pleased to accept a larger income. From the premise that a person is content with the amount of money he has, it cannot be inferred that he would not prefer to have more. It is even possible that he would actually be prepared to sacrifice certain things that he values (e.g., a certain amount of leisure) for the sake of more money.

26. But how can this be compatible with saying that the person is actually content with what he has? What does contentment with a given amount of money preclude, if it does not preclude being ready to make measurable sacrifices in order to obtain more?

What it precludes is having an active interest in getting more. A contented person regards having more money as inessential to his being satisfied with his life.

The fact that he is content is quite consistent with his recognizing that his economic circumstances could be improved, and that his life might as a consequence become better than it is. But this possibility is not important to him. He is simply not much interested in being, so far as money goes, better off than he is. His attention is not vividly engaged by the goods that would be available to him if he had more money. Those goods do not arouse in him any particularly eager or restless concern, although he does acknowledge that he would enjoy additional goods if he had them.

In any event, let us suppose that the level of satisfaction his present monetary circumstances enable him to attain is sufficient to meet his reasonable expectations of life. This is not fundamentally a matter of how much utility or satisfaction his various activities and experiences provide. It is more a matter of his attitude toward being provided with that much. The satisfying experience a person enjoys is one thing. Whether he is satisfied that his life includes just so much satisfaction is another.

Although it is possible that other feasibly attainable circumstances would provide him with greater satisfaction, it may be that he is wholly satisfied with the level of satisfaction he now enjoys. Even if he knows that he could quite possibly obtain even greater satisfaction overall, he does not feel the uneasiness or the ambition that would incline him to seek it. There are quite reasonable people who feel that their lives are good enough, and that it is not important to them whether their lives are as good as possible.[16]

The fact that a person lacks an active interest in getting something does not mean, of course, that he prefers not to have it. The contented person may without any incoherence accept or welcome improvements in his situation; and he may even be prepared to incur minor costs in order to improve it. The fact that he is contented means only that the possibility of improving his situation is not important to him. In other words, it implies only that he does not resent his circumstances, that he is not anxious or determined to improve them, and that he does not go out of his way or undertake any significant initiatives that are designed to make them better.

27. It may seem that there can be no reasonable basis for accepting less satisfaction when one could have more. It may seem, accordingly, that rationality itself entails maximizing, and hence that a person who declines to maximize the level of satisfaction in his life is not being rational. Needless to say, such a person cannot offer as his reason for declining to pursue greater satisfaction an expectation that the costs of that pursuit are likely to be too high; for if that were his reason, then he would be attempting to maximize satisfaction after all. But what other good reason could he possibly have for passing up opportunities for more satisfaction?

In fact, he may have a very good reason for doing so: namely, that he is satisfied with the level of satisfaction he already has. Being satisfied with how things are is clearly an excellent reason for having no great interest in changing them. A person who is satisfied with his life as it is can hardly be criticized, accordingly, on the grounds that he has no good reason for declining to make it better.

Perhaps he might still be open to criticism, on the ground that he should not be satisfied—that it is somehow unreasonable, or unseemly, or in some other mode improper or wrong for him to be satisfied with less satisfaction than he could have. But on what basis could this criticism be justified?

Suppose that a man deeply and happily loves a woman who is altogether worthy. We would not ordinarily criticize the man in such a case just because we thought he might have done even better. Moreover, our sense that it would be inappropriate to criticize him for that reason need not be due simply to a belief that holding out for a more desirable or worthier woman might end up costing him too much.

Rather, it may reflect our recognition that the desire to be happy or content or satisfied with life is a desire for a satisfactory level of satisfaction, and that it is not inherently tantamount to a desire that the level of satisfaction be maximized. Being satisfied with a state of affairs is not equivalent to preferring it to all other possibilities. If someone is faced with an immediate choice between less and more of something he regards as desirable, then perhaps it would be irrational for him to prefer the less to the more. But a person may be satisfied with a given state of affairs without having made any such comparisons.

It is not necessarily irrational or unreasonable for a person to omit or to decline making comparisons between his own circumstances and possible alternatives. This is not only because making such comparisons may be costly. It is also because if someone is satisfied with the way things are, he may have no reasonable motive to consider how they might be otherwise.[17]

28. To be sure, contentment may in some individuals be a function of excessive dullness or diffidence. The fact that a person is free both of resentment and of ambition may be due to his having a slavish character, or it may be due to his vitality being muffled by a kind of negligent lassitude. It is possible for someone to be content merely, as it were, by default.

But a person who is content with resources providing less satisfaction than he could reasonably expect to have may not be irresponsible, or indolent, or deficient in imagination. On the contrary, his decision to be content with his actual resources—in other words, to adopt an attitude of willing acceptance of the fact that he has just that much—may be based upon a conscientiously intelligent and penetrating evaluation of the actual circumstances and quality of his life.

It is not essential for such an evaluation to include an *extrinsic* comparison of the person's circumstances with alternatives to which he might plausibly aspire, as would be necessary if contentment were reasonable only when based upon a judgment that the enjoyment of possible benefits has been maximized. A person may be less interested in whether his circumstances enable him to live as well as possible than he is in whether they enable him to live satisfyingly.

In that case, he may appropriately devote his evaluation entirely to an *intrinsic* appraisal of his life. He may then recognize that his circumstances do not lead him to be resentful or regretful or moved to change, and that—on the basis of his understanding of himself and of what is important to him—he accedes approvingly to a readiness to be content with the way things are. The situation in that event is not so much that he rejects the possibility of improving his circumstances because he thinks there is nothing genuinely to be gained by attempting to improve them. It is rather that this possibility, however feasible it may be, fails as a matter of fact to excite his active attention or to command from him any lively interest.

People often adjust their intentions and their desires to their circumstances. There is a danger that sheer discouragement, or an interest in avoiding frustration and conflict, may lead them to settle for too little. It surely cannot be presumed that someone's life is genuinely fulfilling, or that it is reasonable for the person to be satisfied with it, simply because he is not inclined to complain. On the other hand, it also cannot be presumed that when a person has accommodated his intentions and desires to his circumstances, this is itself evidence that something has gone wrong.

two

equality and respect

1. I propose to deal further, in this section of my book, with issues that pertain to the alleged moral value of equality. So far as I am aware, nothing I shall say concerning these issues implies anything of substance as to the kinds of social or political policies it may be desirable to pursue or to avoid. My discussion is motivated exclusively by conceptual or analytic interests. It is not inspired or shaped by any social or political ideology.

2. I categorically reject the presumption that egalitarianism, of whatever variety, is an ideal of any intrinsic moral importance. This emphatically does not mean that I am inclined generally to endorse or to be indifferent to

prevailing inequalities, or that I oppose efforts to eliminate or to ameliorate them. In fact, I support many such efforts. What leads me to support them, however, is not a conviction that equality of some kind is morally desirable for its own sake and that certain egalitarian goals are therefore inherently worthy. Rather, it is a more contingent and pragmatically grounded belief that in many circumstances greater equality of one sort or another would facilitate the pursuit of other socially or politically desirable aims. I am convinced that equality as such has no inherent or underived moral value at all.[1]

3. Some philosophers believe that an equal distribution of certain valuable resources, just by virtue of being egalitarian, is a significant moral good. Others maintain that what actually is of moral importance is not that the resources be distributed equally but that every-

one enjoy the same level of welfare. All of these philosophers agree that there is some type of equality that is morally valuable in itself, quite apart from whatever utility it may possess in supporting efforts to achieve other morally desirable goals.

It seems to me that insofar as egalitarian ideals are based on the supposition that equality of some kind is morally desirable as such, or for its own sake, the moral appeal of economic egalitarianism is an illusion. It is true that, among morally conscientious individuals, appeals in behalf of equality often have very considerable emotional or rhetorical power. Moreover, as I have indicated, there are situations in which morally pertinent considerations do indeed dictate that a certain inequality should be avoided or reduced. Nevertheless, I believe that it is always a mistake to regard equality of any kind as desirable *inherently*. There is no egalitarian ideal the realization of which is valuable simply and strictly in its own right. Whenever it is morally important to strive for equality, it is always because doing so will promote some other value rather than because equality itself is morally desirable.

In addition to equality of resources and equality of welfare, several other modes of equality may be distinguished: equality of opportunity, equal respect, equal rights, equal consideration, equal concern, and so on. My view is that none of these modes of equality is intrinsically valuable. Hence I maintain that none of the egalitarian ideals corresponding to them has any underived moral worth. Once various conceptual misunderstandings and confusions are dispelled, it appears finally to become clear that equality as such is of no moral importance.

4. With regard to the inegalitarian conditions that prevail when socioeconomic classes

are markedly stratified, Thomas Nagel asks, "How could it not be an evil that some people's life prospects at birth are radically inferior to others'?"[2] The question has undeniable rhetorical force. It seems impossible that any decent person, with normal feelings of human warmth, could fail to recognize that radical initial discrepancies in life prospects are morally unacceptable, and that a readiness to tolerate them would be blatantly immoral.

And yet, is it really indisputable that such discrepancies must always be so awful? Although the life prospects of those in the lower socioeconomic strata have nearly always been terrible, it is not a necessary truth that this familiar relationship must hold. Having less is compatible, after all, with having quite a bit; doing worse than others does not entail doing badly.

It is certainly true that people in the lowest strata of society generally live in horrible conditions. But this association of low social position and dreadful quality of life is not a matter of how things must necessarily be. It is simply a report of how, historically and currently, things generally are. There is no necessary connection between being at the bottom of society and being poor in the sense in which poverty is a serious and morally objectionable barrier to a good life.

Suppose we learn that the prospects of those whose life prospects are "radically inferior" are in fact rather good—not as good as the prospects with which some others begin, of course, but nevertheless good enough to ensure a life that includes many genuinely valuable elements and that people who are both sensitive and reasonable would find deeply satisfying. This is likely to alter the quality of our concern. Even if we should continue to insist that no inequality can ever be fully acceptable, discrepancies between life prospects that are very good and life prospects that are still better may not strike us as warranting the hot sense of moral urgency that is evoked by characterizing every discrepancy of this kind as "evil."

5. The egalitarian condemnation of inequality as inherently bad loses much of its force, I believe, when we recognize that those who are doing considerably worse than others may nonetheless be doing rather well. But the egalitarian position remains misguided even when its moral claims are moderated. Inequality is, after all, a purely formal characteristic; and from this formal characteristic of the relationship between two items, nothing whatever follows as to the desirability or value of either, or of the relationship between them. Surely what is of genuine moral concern is

not *formal* but *substantive*. It is whether people have good lives, and not how their lives compare with the lives of others.

Suppose it is suggested that a life that is radically inferior to others cannot possibly be a good life. It will presumably be conceded that one good life may be less good than another, and hence that mere inferiority does not entail that a life is necessarily bad. It might perhaps be conceded further that this is not entailed even by the fact that the one life is considerably inferior to the other. But suppose someone insists that the very notion of being radically inferior entails not merely that a life is less good than others, but that the life falls decisively below the threshold that separates lives that are good from lives that are not good.

Let it be accepted as a conceptually necessary truth, then, that radically inferior lives are invariably bad. In that case, it will be entirely reasonable to agree that the radical inferiority of some people's life prospects is indeed—as Nagel says—an evil. But why is it an evil? The evil does not lie in the circumstance that the inferior lives happen to be unequal to other lives. What makes it an evil that certain people have bad lives is not that some other people have better lives. The evil lies simply in the conspicuous fact that bad lives are bad.

6. When someone is wondering whether to be satisfied with the resources at his disposal, or when he is evaluating the level of his well-being, what is it genuinely important for him to take into account? The assessments he wishes to make are personal; they have to do with the specific quality of his own life. What he must do, it seems clear, is to make these assessments on the basis of a realistic estimate of how closely the course of his life suits his individual capacities, meets his particular needs,

fulfills his best potentialities, and provides him with what he himself cares about.

With respect to none of these considerations, it seems to me, is it essential for him to measure his circumstances against the circumstances of anyone else. No doubt, such comparisons may often be illuminating; they may enable a person to understand his own situation more clearly. Even so, they are at best helpful. They do not get to the heart of the matter.

If a person has enough resources to provide for the satisfaction of his needs and his interests, his resources are then entirely adequate; their adequacy does not depend in addition on the magnitude of the resources other people possess. Whether the opportunities available to a person include the alternatives from which it would be desirable for him to be able to choose depends on what opportunities suit his capacities, his interests, and his potentialities. It does not depend on whether his opportunities coincide with those that are available to others.

The same goes for rights, for respect, for consideration, and for concern. Enjoying the rights that it is appropriate for a person to enjoy, and being treated with appropriate consideration and concern, have nothing essentially to do with the consideration and concern that other people are shown or with the respect or rights that other people happen to enjoy. Every person should be accorded the rights, the respect, the consideration, and the concern to which he is entitled by virtue of what he is and what he has done. The extent of his entitlement to them does not depend on whether or not other people are entitled to them as well.[3]

It may be that the entitlements of all people to certain things are in fact the same. If this were to be so, however, it would not be because equality is important. Rather, it would be because all people happen to be the same, or are necessarily the same, with regard to the characteristics from which the entitlements in question derive—for instance, common humanity, a capacity for suffering, citizenship in the kingdom of ends, or whatever. The mere fact that one person has something or is entitled to something—taken simply by itself—is no reason at all for another person to want the same thing or to think himself entitled to it. In other words, equality as such has no moral importance.

7. Still, this is not the end of the story. Consider someone who is in no way concerned about equality for its own sake, and who is also quite satisfied that he has as much of everything as he can use, but who happens to have less of certain things than others have. The fact that he has been treated unequally

might offend him, even though he does not object to inequality as such. He might consider the inequality between his condition and the condition of others to be objectionable because it might suggest to him that whoever is responsible for the discrepancy has failed to treat him with a certain kind of respect.

It is easy to confuse being treated with the sort of respect in question with being treated equally. However, the two are not the same. I believe that the widespread tendency to exaggerate the moral importance of egalitarianism is due, at least in part, to a misunderstanding of the relationship between treating people equally and treating them with respect.

The most fundamental difference between equality and respect has to do with focus and intent. With regard to any interesting parameter—whether it pertains to resources, welfare, opportunity, rights, consideration, concern, or whatever—equality is merely a matter of each person's having the same as others. Respect is more personal. Treating a person with respect means, in the sense that is germane here, dealing with him exclusively on the basis of those aspects of his particular character or circumstances that are actually relevant to the issue at hand.

Treating people with respect precludes assigning them special advantages or disadvantages, except on the basis of considerations that differentiate them relevantly from those to whom those advantages or disadvantages are not assigned. Thus it entails impartiality and the avoidance of arbitrariness. Those who are concerned with equality aim at outcomes that are in some pertinent way indistinguishable. On the other hand, those who wish to treat people with respect aim at outcomes matched specifically to the particularities of the individual. It is clear that the direction in which a desire for dealing equally points may diverge from the direction in which an interest in showing respect and acting impartially will lead.[4]

8. Under certain circumstances, to be sure, the requirements of equality and of respect will converge. It is important that this convergence not be misconstrued.

Consider a situation in which no information is available either about any relevant similarities between two people or about any relevant differences between them. In that case, the most natural and the most sensible recourse is to treat both people the same—that is, to treat them equally. The fact that an egalitarian policy is the only plausible one under such conditions may give rise to an impression that a preference for equality is—as it were—the default position, which must be implemented in the absence of considerations showing that an alternative is required.

Many thinkers do in fact claim that egalitarianism enjoys a presumptive moral advantage over other policies. In their view, it is always desirable for equality to prevail unless the initial moral superiority of an egalitarian policy is overcome by particular features of the situation at hand.

Isaiah Berlin is among those who advance this view, as follows:

> The assumption is that equality needs no reasons, only inequality does so.... If I have a cake and there are ten persons among whom I wish to divide it, then if I give exactly one tenth to each, this will not, at any rate automatically, call for justification; whereas if I depart from this principle of equal division I am expected to produce a special reason.[5]

This sort of account appeals to many people; indeed, it is widely thought to be confirmed by elementary common sense. In fact, however, the assumption Berlin enunciates is mistaken. Equality has no inherent moral advantage over inequality. There is no basis for a presumption in favor of egalitarian goals.

If it would in fact be morally correct to distribute Berlin's cake in equal shares, the explanation is not, as he supposes, that equality needs no reasons, or that egalitarian distribution enjoys an initial moral superiority over other alternatives. The critical feature of the situation he imagines is that he has neither a special reason for dividing the cake equally nor a special reason for dividing it unequally. In other words, the situation is one in which he does not know either that the people among whom the cake is to be divided are alike in ways that warrant giving them equal shares or that they differ in ways that justify giving them shares of different sizes. He has no relevant information about these people at all.

This means, of course, that the relevant information available to him about each of the people is exactly the same: namely, zero. But if his relevant information about each person is identical with his information about the others—as it would be, of course, if he actually has no information—it would be arbitrary and disrespectful to treat the people differently; impartiality requires that he treat everyone the same. So he does have a reason that justifies an egalitarian distribution of the cake. It is the moral importance of respect, and hence of impartiality, rather than of any supposedly prior or preemptive moral importance of equality, that constrains us to treat people the same when we know nothing that provides us with a special reason for treating them differently.

In cases like the one Berlin describes, it is merely a happenstance that the requirements of equality and of respect coincide. There may also be circumstances in which the coincidence of these requirements is not so contingent. Suppose we agree that everyone is entitled to certain things just in virtue of being human. With regard to these entitlements, individual differences naturally cannot provide any relevant basis for differentiating between one person and another; for the only characteristics of each person that are relevant—to wit, simply those that constitute his humanity— are necessarily shared by every other human being. Therefore, the criteria of impartiality and of equality must inescapably yield, in this case, the same result.

The fact that this sort of case requires equality is not grounded, however, in any moral authority that egalitarianism possesses in its own right. Rather, the claim of egalitarianism is derivative. It is grounded in the more basic requirements of respect and of impartiality. What most fundamentally dictates that all human beings must be accorded the same entitlements is the presumed moral importance of responding impartially to their common humanity, and not any alleged moral importance of equality as an independently compelling goal.

9. What is it about impartiality, and about what I have been referring to as "respect," that makes them morally imperative? Why is it important to be guided in dealing with people only by whatever it is about them that is genuinely relevant? There is a sense in which being guided by what is relevant—thus treating similar cases alike and relevantly unlike cases differently—is an elementary aspect of being rational.[6] It might be suggested, accordingly, that the moral value of these ways of treating people derives from the importance of avoiding the irrationality that would be entailed by relying on irrelevancies. But this only raises

another question. What is the moral importance of avoiding irrationality?

10. It is desirable that people be rational. On the other hand, this does not mean that irrationality as such is immoral. The fact that adopting a certain belief or pursuing a certain course of behavior contravenes the requirements of rationality does not entail that a moral imperative of some kind has been violated. People who reason imperfectly are surely not, just on that account, morally culpable. So there must be something else about deviations from respect, besides the fact that they are breaches of rationality, that has a more immediate and a more specific moral import.

People who resent disrespectful treatment do so because, by its very nature, it conveys a refusal to acknowledge the truth about them.[7] Failing to respect someone is a matter of ignoring the relevance of some aspect of his nature or of his situation. The lack of respect consists in the circumstance that some important fact about the person is not properly attended to or is not appropriately taken into account. In other words, the person is dealt with as though he is not what he actually is. The implications of significant features of his life are overlooked or denied. Pertinent aspects of how things are with him are treated as though they had no reality. When he is denied suitable respect, it is as though his very existence is reduced.

This sort of treatment, at least when it has to do with matters of some consequence, may naturally evoke painful feelings of resentment. It may also evoke a more or less inchoate anxiety; for when a person is treated as though significant elements of his life count for nothing, it is natural for him to experience this as in a certain way an assault on his reality. What is at stake for him, when people act as though he is not what he is, is a kind of self-preservation. It is not his biological survival that is challenged, of course, when his nature is denied. It is the reality of his existence for others, and hence the solidity of his own sense that he himself is real.

11. Experiences of being ignored—of not being taken seriously, of not counting, of being unable to make one's presence felt or one's voice heard—may be profoundly disturbing. They often trigger in people an extraordinarily protective response, which may be quite incommensurate in its intensity with the magnitude of the damage to their objective interests that is actually threatened. The classic articulation of this response is in the limitlessly reckless cry to "let justice be done, though the heavens may fall."

What leads to such an unmeasured and perhaps even self-destructive demand for redress is plainly not a deliberate appraisal of the extent of the injustice that has been done, nor is it a careful estimate of what it might actually take to undo the injustice. The demand issues in a less calculated manner from the unbearably deep suffering and dread that may be caused when people are treated unjustly—that is, when their personal reality is threatened by a denial of the importance that is required by respect.

Demands for equality have a very different meaning in our lives than do demands for respect. Someone who insists that he be treated equally is calculating his demands on the basis of what other people have rather than on the basis of what will accord with the realities of his own condition and will most suitably provide for his own interests and needs. In his desire for equality, there is no affirmation by a person of himself. On the contrary, a concern for simply being equal to others leads people to define their goals in terms that are set by

considerations other than the specific requirements of their own distinctive nature and of
their own circumstances. It tends to distract
them from recognizing their most authentic
ambitions, which are those that derive from
the character of their own lives, and not those
that are imposed on them by the conditions
in which others happen to live.

Needless to say, the pursuit of egalitarian
goals often has very substantial utility in promoting a variety of compelling political and
social ideals. But the widespread conviction
that equality itself and as such has some basic
value as an independently important moral
ideal is not only mistaken. It is an impedi-
ment to the identification of what is truly of
fundamental moral and social worth.

acknowledgments

Portions of this book were originally published in a somewhat different form as "Equality as a Moral Ideal," *Ethics* 98, no. 1 (October 1987): 21–43; and "Equality and Respect," *Social Research* 64, no. 1 (Spring 1997): 3–15, copyright © 1997 by The New School for Social Research, reprinted with permission by Johns Hopkins University Press.

notes

preface

1. See Thomas Piketty, *Capital in the Twenty-First Century* (Cambridge, MA: Harvard University Press, 2014).

one: economic equality as a moral ideal

1. The moral and psychological problems arising from the fact that some people have too much are eminently worthy of study and analysis. This book focuses, however, on the more pressing phenomenon of people who have too little.

2. This version of economic egalitarianism might also be formulated as the doctrine that there should be no inequalities in the distribution of money. The

two formulations are not unambiguously equivalent, because the term "distribution" is equivocal. It may refer either to a pattern of possession or to an activity of allocation, and there are significant differences in the criteria for evaluating "distributions" in the two senses.

3. Thomas Nagel writes: "The defense of economic equality on the ground that it is needed to protect political, legal and social equality ... [is not] a defense of equality *per se*—equality in the possession of benefits in general. Yet the latter is a further moral idea of great importance. Its validity would provide an independent reason to favor economic equality as a good in its own right" ("Equality," in his *Mortal Questions* [Cambridge: Cambridge University Press, 1979], p. 107).

4. I focus attention here especially on the standard of equality in the distribution of money, chiefly in order to facilitate my discussion of the standard of sufficiency. Many egalitarians, to be sure, consider equality to be morally important in certain other matters as well: e.g., welfare, satisfaction of needs, opportunity, respect. I believe that some of what I have to say about economic egalitarianism and sufficiency does apply also to these other goods; but I

shall not attempt in this essay to define the scope of its applicability. Nor shall I attempt to relate my views to other recent criticisms of egalitarianism (e.g., Larry S. Temkin, "Inequality," *Philosophy and Public Affairs* 13 [1986]: 99–121; Robert E. Goodin, "Epiphenomenal Egalitarianism," *Social Research* 52 [1985]: 99–117).

5. Formulations and discussions of the argument are in Kenneth Arrow, "A Utilitarian Approach to the Concept of Equality in Public Expenditures," *Quarterly Journal of Economics* 85 (1971): 409–10; Walter Blum and Harry Kalven, *The Uneasy Case for Progressive Taxation* (Chicago: University of Chicago Press, 1966); Abba Lerner, *The Economics of Control* (New York: Macmillan Publishing Co., 1944); Paul Samuelson, *Economics* (New York: McGraw-Hill Book Co., 1972), pp. 431–34; and "A. P. Lerner at Sixty," in *Collected Scientific Papers of Paul A. Samuelson*, ed. Robert C. Merton, 3 vols. (Cambridge, MA: MIT Press, 1972), 3:643–52. Arrow says, "In the utilitarian discussion of income distribution, equality of income is derived from the maximization conditions if it is further assumed that individuals have the same utility functions, each with diminishing marginal utility" ("Utilitarian Approach," p. 409). Samuelson

offers the following formulation: "If each extra dollar brings less and less satisfaction to a man, and if the rich and poor are alike in their capacity to enjoy satisfaction, a dollar taxed away from a millionaire and given to a median-income person is supposed to add more to total utility than it subtracts" (*Economics*, p. 164, n. 1).

6. In other words: (a) the utility provided by or derivable from an nth dollar is, for everyone, less than the utility of the dollar acquired just previously— i.e., for any dollar n, $U(n) > U(n - 1)$; and (b) the comparative utilities of various items are the same for everyone.

7. This relationship between redistribution and inflation has been explained to me (in correspondence) by Professor Richard Robb of Columbia University's Department of Economics.

8. "With successive new units of a good, your total utility will grow at a slower and slower rate because of a fundamental tendency for your psychological ability to appreciate more of the good to become less keen. This fact, that the increments in total utility fall off, economists describe as follows: As the amount consumed of a good increases, the marginal utility of the good (or the extra utility added by its

last unit) tends to decrease" (Samuelson, *Economics*, p. 431).

9. Lerner, *The Economics of Control*, pp. 26–27.

10. There are two possibilities here. Suppose on the one hand that, instead of obtaining $G(n)$ when his income is n dollars, the rational consumer saves that money until he can add an additional i dollars to it and then purchases $G(n + i)$. In this case, having deferred the purchase of $G(n + i)$ obviously does not mean that it is valued less than $G(n)$.

On the other hand, suppose that the rational consumer declines to save up for $G(n + i)$, and that he spends all his money on obtaining $G(n)$. In this case too it is not true that his behavior indicates the preference that Lerner presumes. For the explanation of the consumer's refusal to save for $G(n + i)$ may be merely that he regards doing so as pointless because he believes that he cannot reasonably expect to save enough to obtain it within an acceptable period of time.

The utility of $G(n + i)$ may also be greater than the sum of the utilities of $G(n)$ and $G(i)$. That is, in acquiring $G(n + i)$, the consumer may cross a utility threshold. In such a case, the income of the rational consumer does not exhibit diminishing marginal utility.

11. Conditions of these kinds are discussed in N. Rescher, *Distributive Justice* (Indianapolis: Bobbs-Merrill Co., 1966), pp. 28–30.

12. It might be correct to say that a person actually does need one unit of a resource, even though the resource is lifesaving only if the person has five units. That might be the case if there is a chance that he will somehow receive four more units. The one unit might then be regarded as being, at least potentially, an integral constituent of the total of five units that will put him across the threshold of survival. But if there is no possibility that he will acquire five, acquiring the one is not enough to contribute to the satisfaction of any need.

13. Ronald Dworkin presents a typical example of the confusion of equality and sufficiency. He characterizes the ideal of economic equality as requiring that "no citizen has less than an equal share of the community's resources just in order that others may have more of what he lacks." In support of his claim that the United States now falls short of this ideal, however, he refers to circumstances that are evidence not primarily of inequality but of insufficiency or poverty. Thus: "It is, I think, apparent that the United States falls far short now [of the ideal of equality]. A

substantial minority of Americans are chronically unemployed, or earn wages below any realistic 'poverty line'" ("Why Liberals Should Care about Equality," in *A Matter of Principle* [Cambridge, MA: Harvard University Press, 1985], p. 208).

14. In the second essay in this book, I suggest another possible source of moral uneasiness at the spectacle of inequality.

15. Within the limits of this essay, it makes no difference which view is taken concerning the very important question of whether what counts is the attitude a person actually has or the attitude it would be reasonable for him to have.

16. It is gratuitous to assume that every reasonable person must be seeking to maximize the benefits he can obtain, in a sense requiring that he be endlessly interested in or open to improving his life. A certain deviation from economic equality might be against someone's interest, because it might be that he would in fact be better off without it. But as long as it does not conflict with his interest, by obstructing his opportunity to lead the sort of life that it is truly important for him to lead, the deviation from equality may be morally quite innocent and acceptable. To be wholly satisfied with a certain state of affairs, a

reasonable person need not suppose that there is no other available state of affairs in which he would be better off.

17. Compare the rather sensible adage: "If it ain't broke, don't fix it."

two: equality and respect

1. In the introduction to their anthology *Equality: Selected Readings* (New York: Oxford University Press, 1997), Louis Pojman and Robert Westmoreland attribute to me the view that, with regard to economic considerations, "in an affluent society we have a duty to provide for people's minimal needs, but nothing further" (p. 11). That is by no means my view. In the first essay in the present volume, entitled "Economic Equality as a Moral Ideal," I argue that what is morally important is not that people have equal incomes or equal wealth but that each person have enough. By "enough," as I attempted to make clear, I meant enough for a good life, not—as Pojman and Westmoreland suppose—merely enough to get by.

2. Thomas Nagel, *Equality and Partiality* (New York: Oxford University Press, 1991), p. 28.

3. In *Inequality Reexamined* (Cambridge, MA: Harvard University Press, 1992), Amartya Sen claims that "to have any kind of plausibility, ethical reasoning on social matters must involve elementary equal consideration for all at some level that is seen as critical" (p. 17). But what does "equal consideration" mean? Surely giving young people equal consideration does not mean spending equal time or equal effort in considering their interests or their entitlements. Sen himself suggests that it has to do with avoiding arbitrariness: "the absence of such equality would make a theory arbitrarily discriminating and hard to defend" (ibid.). But avoiding arbitrariness has nothing to do with treating people equally. It is a matter of having a reasonable basis for treating them as one does. It would be arbitrarily discriminating to give greater consideration to one person than to another, without having a reasonable basis for discriminating between them; and it would similarly be arbitrary to give both the same consideration, when there is a reasonable basis for treating them differently. To avoid arbitrariness, we must treat likes alike and unlikes differently. This is no more an egalitarian principle than it is an inegalitarian one.

4. Since the value assigned to respect may be overridden by other values, people often prefer—sometimes for perfectly good or even admirable reasons—to be treated as though they have characteristics they do not have or as though they lack characteristics they actually possess. I recognize that it is rather dissonant to characterize such people, as I imply here, as trying to avoid being treated respectfully. A disinclination to appear and to be treated as what one is may sometimes but not always, perhaps, suggest a lack of self-respect. I have been unable to design a more suitable terminology.

5. Isaiah Berlin, "Equality as an Ideal," *Proceedings of the Aristotelian Society* 56 (1955–56): 132; reprinted in *Justice and Social Policy*, ed. Frederick Olafson (Englewood Cliffs, NJ: Prentice-Hall, 1961).

6. What counts as relevant and what counts as irrelevant may often depend heavily, of course, on moral considerations.

7. Earlier, I indicated that people may sometimes welcome being treated without respect. This would presumably be because they had reason to conceal or to misrepresent the truth about themselves. In what follows, I shall be considering only cases in which disrespectful treatment is in fact resented.